KHMER ROUGE ABUSES ALONG THE

THAI-CAMBODIAN BORDER

An Asia Watch Report
February   1989

Cover design by Lolette Guthrie

CONTENTS

INTRODUCTION

Between June and November 1988 the Khmer Rouge attempted to move up to 15,000 Cambodian refugees* from camps under Khmer Rouge administration inside Thailand to combat zones close to or inside Cambodia. The apparent aim was to set up bases for military operations against the Vietnamese-supported People's Republic of Kampuchea (PRK) as Vietnamese troops withdrew.

Intensive shelling by Vietnamese forces prevented the achievement of that aim, and many of the refugees were caught in the no man's land between the Thai border and Vietnamese defense lines just inside Cambodia. It is an area made lethal by the estimated half million mines placed there by the armed forces of Thailand, Vietnam, and the three Cambodian resistance factions** and by widespread malaria that in the absence of medical treatment is frequently fatal.

The fate of the displaced refugees is not clear. Some were driven back to the refugee camps. Some died in the shelling. Most remain unaccounted for.

They were not the only victims. In moving all able-bodied men, women and children, together with food, water, medical and housing supplies from selected camps, the Khmer Rouge left behind all those deemed to have no further military or political use. They abandoned the aged and infirm together with a large number of paraplegics maimed by land mines while undertaking forced labor for the Khmer Rouge as porters of arms and ammunition into Cambodia.

The attempted forced repatriation was a violation of international human rights standards and laws regulating armed conflict. The

---

* The word "refugee" is used throughout this report, even though the Thai government has not granted legal refugee status to most of the Cambodians in Thailand.

** Far Eastern Economic Review, December 1, 1988.

1

fundamental distinction between civilians and combatants upon which the Geneva Conventions rest was not observed. The population removals constituted cruel and inhuman treatment of those forced into the war zone. The principle that the wounded and sick should be cared for was violated, both by denying those injured in the shelling access to medical care and by leaving behind without adequate treatment those not well enough to make the move.

The population removals of late 1988, together with the documented pattern of systematic human rights abuses in Khmer Rouge-controlled camps and the determination to keep refugees away from the "contaminating" influence of Western and international aid agencies, are chillingly reminiscent of the barbarous practices that characterized Khmer Rouge rule in Cambodia from 1975-1979.

The apparently unchanged policies of the Khmer Rouge underscore the need for the international community to ensure that any negotiated settlement include workable safeguards for the protection of the human rights of the Cambodian people. The Khmer Rouge appear determined to play a major role in Cambodia whatever the settlement reached.

If it is not clear that its forces will triumph after Vietnamese forces withdraw from the country, it is clear from its efforts to establish military bases inside Cambodia that it is committed to waging both guerrilla war and political struggle for years to come.

This report, based largely on interviews with refugees and aid officials conducted along the border by Asia Watch consultant Mary Kay Magistad in November 1988, summarizes the extent of available information on the forced removal of refugees in late 1988 against the backdrop of diplomatic moves in Paris, Jakarta, Hanoi, Beijing and Moscow towards a resolution of the Cambodian conflict. It documents case studies of human rights violations by the Khmer Rouge in camps they administer. And it concludes with recommendations on safeguards that might prevent a repetition of the past.

The report does not address human rights violations in refugee camps controlled by other resistance factions nor those for which the Phnom Penh-based People's Republic of Kampuchea (PRK) government is responsible. These issues have been addressed in recent reports of the Lawyers Committee for Human Rights and

2

Amnesty International. Asia Watch believes that the past record of the Khmer Rouge and the prospects of its involvement in a post-settlement government warrant particular attention to its current human rights violations.

Ms. Magistad is the primary author of this report. David Hawk, who conducted interviews in Thailand and Cambodia for Asia Watch in November 1988, also contributed.

POLITICAL   BACKGROUND

The Khmer Rouge are best known and feared for their brutal policies that led to the deaths -- by murder, starvation or sheer exhaustion -- of more than one million of their fellow Cambodians between 1975 and 1979.

After seizing power from the American-backed Lon Nol regime in April 1975, the Khmer Rouge emptied Cambodia's cities.   They declared a return to "Year Zero" and started a campaign to purge Cambodia of all "corrupting" influences, resulting in the execution of hundreds of thousands of civil servants, professionals, teachers, monks, peasants, members of minority groups and others.

With Pol Pot at the helm of the government called Democratic Kampuchea, the Khmer Rouge forged a tightly regimented society in which the majority of Cambodians were forced to work 16-hour days in the fields on starvation rations, where children were taught to spy on their parents and turn them in for "counter-revolutionary" activities, and where individual human rights were all but extinguished.

In December 1978 Vietnamese troops swept into Cambodia, driving out the Khmer Rouge and establishing the People's Republic of Kampuchea (PRK) in January 1979.

The Vietnamese invasion had major international repercussions. Neither China nor Thailand was prepared to accept a *fait   accompli* by Vietnam in Cambodia.   China invaded Vietnam in December 1979 to "teach it a lesson."   Thailand helped funnel arms and aid from China to the Khmer Rouge.

One immediate impact was the large-scale influx of Cambodian refugees into Thailand. Over 150,000 Cambodians obtained political asylum in refugee facilities administered by the United Nations High Commissioner for Refugees (UNHCR).   Hundreds of thousands more massed along the Thai-Cambodian border.   By 1985, Vietnamese attacks had pushed those Cambodians into Thailand.   By 1988, there were over 300,000 refugees in camps along the border serviced by international aid agencies including the special United Nations agen-

5

cy established for the purpose, the United Nations Border Relief Operation (UNBRO).

At the same time as large concentrations of refugees were filling camps in Thailand, different Cambodian factions opposed to Vietnamese rule began to emerge with their political bases in those camps. In October 1979, the anti-communist Khmer People's /National Liberation Front (KPNLF) was formed under the leadership of former Prime Minister Son Sann. In 1981 groups loyal to Prince Norodom Sihanouk set up the United Front for an Independent, Neutral, Peaceful and Cooperative Cambodia (FUNCINPEC) which was also anti-communist.

The Khmer Rouge survived their expulsion from Cambodia thanks to a steady supply of arms from Vietnam's traditional enemy, China, delivered to the Khmer Rouge by Thai forces who wanted a buffer against the Vietnamese.* To facilitate that supply in light of the widespread condemnation of Pol Pot's policies, the countries of the Association of Southeast Asian Nations (ASEAN) -- Thailand, Malaysia, Singapore, Indonesia and the Philippines -- took the lead in forging the three resistance factions into the Coalition Government of Democratic Kampuchea (CGDK) in 1982. As part of the CGDK, the Khmer Rouge could continue to fight the Vietnamese in the name of Prince Sihanouk and retain Democratic Kampuchea's seat at the United Nations.

The CGDK won overwhelming support at the United Nations, not only from ASEAN, but also from the Western democracies, Japan, the Islamic bloc and many non-aligned countries eager to have a shield against the further expansion of Soviet influence in Asia, especially after the invasion of Afghanistan.

Much of the international support for the CGDK and the Khmer Rouge role within it was predicated on the assumption of a continuing Vietnamese presence in Cambodia. Until 1988 no one took seriously the periodic claims by Vietnam that it had withdrawn troops

---

* There also appears to have been a trade-off whereby the Chinese agreed to stop supporting the Thai communist insurgency if the Thais helped the Khmer Rouge.

from Cambodia. These were widely regarded as staged rotations of the military units.

But the international politics of the region have changed dramatically in the last year. CGDK and PRK leaders have held a series of talks in Paris and Jakarta about a possible settlement involving the three resistance factions and the ruling party of the PRK, the People's Revolutionary Party of Kampuchea. The United Nations is actively seeking a settlement. Relations between the Soviet Union and China have improved, leading to pressure from Moscow on the Vietnamese to withdraw in exchange for an as yet unrealized commitment from China to halt arms supplies to the Khmer Rouge. Talks on resolving the Cambodian conflict accelerated in January 1989 between China and Vietnam.

The Vietnamese withdrawal is now taking place, and the future role of the Khmer Rouge in Cambodia is becoming an issue of international concern. The attempt in late 1988 to force refugees back into Cambodia seems to demonstrate that the Khmer Rouge are intent on continuing the armed struggle to take control of the country, regardless of whatever settlement is negotiated by other parties to the conflict. The U.S. Defense Department testified during a Congressional hearing in July 1988 that the Khmer Rouge had stockpiled up to two years' worth of Chinese-supplied weapons inside Cambodia. And one refugee who escaped from a Khmer Rouge camp closed to international aid agencies, on the southern Thai-Cambodian border, told journalists in October 1988 that he fled because the Khmer Rouge had told him and other refugees they would soon be moved back into Cambodia and would be "the vanguard of the new revolution."

LACK OF ACCESS TO
KHMER ROUGE-CONTROLLED CAMPS

As of January 1989, the United Nations Border Relief Operation (UNBRO) listed 287,334 refugees as receiving UN aid on the Thai-Cambodian border. Of these, 46,025 were living in camps administered by the Khmer Rouge.* Aid officials acknowledge, however, that at least the same number live in Khmer Rouge-controlled camps beyond their reach. Refugees in those camps are at the mercy of camp administrators who reportedly vary in the degree of control they exercise. Many, if not most, of the refugees are believed to be in Khmer Rouge camps against their will; escaped residents of Khmer Rouge camps interviewed by Asia Watch indicated that many refugees stumbled into Khmer Rouge camps by accident while trying to reach camps controlled by other factions or fell into Khmer Rouge hands in Cambodia before they reached the border. A mixture of tight control and fear prevent more refugees from trying to escape.

Without access by international relief and humanitarian agencies, there are few safeguards against abuses by camp authorities. Thailand has not insisted on such access, although the closed camps are on Thai soil, and Khmer Rouge forces are dependent on the Thai military for delivery of food and weapons. On the contrary, Thai authorities have actively cooperated with the Khmer Rouge and have been unwilling or unable to prevent forced portering and other abuses. Recent steps, however, suggest that the Thai government may be beginning to play a more positive role. In late 1988 they began to station a specially-trained force called the Displaced Persons Protection Unit in the four Khmer Rouge camps which receive UNBRO aid, providing some protection to refugees there. In addition, they

---

* These figures do not include the 6,000 refugees at O'Trao, a camp which re-opened at the end of January 1989 and which also receives UNBRO aid.

9

appeared as of mid-February 1989 to be moving toward a plan that would draw refugees out of the closed camps to those served by international agencies. It is not clear how this plan would be implemented.

At present, international aid agencies have access to only four Khmer Rouge camps: Site 8, Ta Luan, O'Trao and Borai. O'Trao, on the northeastern border, was closed for most of January after disgruntled elements of the Khmer Rouge there, reportedly upset with UNBRO's direct delivery of food to the camp, burned down the camp hospital on December 24. Thai military officials closed the camp for "security reasons," according to Asia Watch sources, but allowed it to reopen at the end of January. It now has an estimated population of 6,000. Until June 1988 when Khmer Rouge cadre began to move some 5,000 to 9,000 refugees to "satellite" camps close to the border, O'Trao's population was estimated at 16,000 to 21,000. Thai military officials on the border have confirmed that while the camp was closed in January, its population dipped to 2,000, suggesting that further population removals took place.

Among the camps to which aid agencies have no access are the satellite camps around O'Trao, such as Ban Chankor (exact population unknown but thought to be growing because of transfers of refugees from O'Trao); Ban Charat (about 20 kilometers from Site B and thought to be a major military center and land-bridge to Cambodia for the Khmer Rouge); Aou Panko (a camp hugging the border with a population estimated at close to 3,000, thought to have been the target of heavy shelling from the PRK and Vietnamese in November 1988); Nougva (a little-known camp almost on top of the border near the Thai village of Ban Dan); and Samrong Kiat (population estimated at 1,500).

The same "satellite" system of closed camps also exists on the southern border, in the Ta Luan-Borai area. Khmer Rouge officials in Ta Luan have said they oversee some 17,000 refugees in the region, but only 5,000 to 6,000 of these are accessible to international aid agencies. Others are (or have been) in such camps as Kai Che, V3 and O'Trao South.

Even the "showcase" camp of Site 8, to which the press has access, is surrounded by closed satellites. One of these is the top-security Site 8 North, also known as Phnom Dey, with a population of 5,000 to 6,000. This camp, which can be seen from the road between the Thai border town of Aranyaprathet and Site 8, seems to double as a re-education camp and prison for those who criticize the Khmer Rouge line or appear "counter-revolutionary".

Another camp near Site 8 is Site 8 West, also known as Site 85 (population thought to be between 10,000 and 12,000), to which refugees are said to be sent for indoctrination and military training. Finally, there is Site 8 South, with a population of about 4,000, which aid sources say appears to be a highly sensitive and strategic military camp.

The difficulty in determining exact numbers of refugees in some of the closed camps is exacerbated by the Khmer Rouge practice of naming their camps by numbers as well as by the names by which they are known to outsiders. Thus, Ta Luan is also known as V4; the now-closed camp of Huay Chan was also called Site 1001; and the camp of Natrao (now closed as well) was known as Site 40. In May 1988, the Khmer Rouge moved the refugees in these two camps, reportedly at the request of Thai officials who wanted to develop the land on which the camps were based. Most of the Natrao refugees went to O'Trao (also known as Camp 1003), while Huay Chan refugees are thought to have moved to Ban Chankor and other satellite camps. The UN lost access to these refugees after it cut off food supplies to Huay Chan in May 1988. The cut-off was a response to the Khmer Rouge refusal to allow UN officials access to the camp to monitor distribution.

THE FORCED REMOVALS OF 1988

The Khmer Rouge forced thousands of people to leave Ta Luan and O'Trao camps in the latter half of 1988. It is significant that aid officials had at least partial access to both camps, and they told Asia Watch that without such access, they would not have found out that the population movements had taken place.

"We only know about these movements because we've been allowed to visit these camps on a semi-regular basis and can see when the situation changes," said one aid official at the border. "For all we know, this sort of thing could have been going on for months or years already. And we haven't a clue what's happening in the camps out of our reach. There may be many more involuntary movements of refugees--movements that put their safety at risk -- that we just don't know about."

Ta Luan Camp

Between June and September 1988, Khmer Rouge cadre loaded between 7,000 and 8,000 of Ta Luan's 9,000 refugees onto Chinese-supplied military trucks and transported them -- along with the thatch and bamboo from UNBRO-supplied homes -- to forward positions closer to or inside the Cambodian border. Even papaya trees from the camp were uprooted and taken along.

Aid agency officials believe the move may have been an attempt by the Khmer Rouge to isolate the refugees from Western influence as well as to establish base camps inside Cambodia for use in future infiltration.

The refugees, the majority of whom were apparently women and children, were taken to sites which the Khmer Rouge call "repatriation villages". In fact they are reportedly little more than temporary shelters with no amenities or medical facilities. The *Far Eastern Economic Review* reported that aid officials who had visited Ta Luan found that only sick people of proven loyalty to the Khmer Rouge were allowed to return to Ta Luan for treatment.*

A group of teen-aged children caught up in the forced displacement and who later returned to Ta Luan told a recent visitor there that camp commanders told them they were being moved because the mines around the camp had made it too dangerous. They were not told where they were being moved and did not ask. To them, the move seemed no different than earlier incidents where they were ordered to carry supplies across the border.

When concerned aid officials questioned the refugees' disappearance, the Khmer Rouge told them in effect that it was none of their business. But the aid officials declared a medical emergency there on August 27, 1988 upon finding "180 patients, 45 of them seriously ill, and a 15-year-old medic in charge," according to an Associated Press report.

By September, fewer than 2,000 remained in Ta Luan. The AP report described those left behind as "the crippled, the blind, the amputees, the worthless people, the waste of the operation."

The amputees alone numbered some 500. Almost all were victims of land mine explosions, often from accidents which occurred while carrying ammunition into Cambodia.

O'Trao

The displacement from O'Trao was similar. In early October 1988, 5,000 to 9,000 refugees were moved from the camp--between one-fourth and one-third of its total population. The numbers are vague because aid workers estimate that 5,000 to 6,000 O'Trao residents were not registered for UNBRO food rations and thus not included in the official population figures. (O'Trao is also an extremely difficult camp in which to take a proper census. Small clusters of huts

---

* See The New York Times, November 13, 1988 and Far Eastern Economic Review, December 1, 1988.

are dotted in the jungle, surrounded by trees and thick brush. The camp residents are rarely together in any central place.)

The refugees were transported in trucks belonging to a Thai military unit called Task Force 838, according to the *Far Eastern Economic Review*, and were taken to three satellite camps near the border.[*] When aid officials asked about the move, after noticing gaping holes in the jungle where groups of houses used to be, the Khmer Rouge told them that the missing refugees were simply soldiers and their families who had moved nearer the border. They insisted that the refugees had moved voluntarily because they "want to go home."

Among those left behind at O'Trao were all of the amputees in the camp. They were living together in a colony, separated from the rest of the camp by a Khmer Rouge target practice range.

---

*   Far Eastern Economic Review, December 1, 1988.

PREVIOUS FORCED REMOVALS

The 1988 displacements were by no means the first. In August 1985, the Khmer Rouge trucked some 5,000 civilians to the military camp called Site 8 North, also known as Phnom Dey, a camp closed to foreigners. Most of those transferred were said to be relatives of soldiers. But at least some were moved at gunpoint, according to The Lawyers Committee for Human Rights. In their 1986 report *Seeking Shelter*, the Committee noted that some of the Cambodians relocated to Phnom Dey appeared to have been transferred from there into Cambodia.

The report said another 1,500 residents of the Khmer Rouge-controlled Samrong Kiat camp also seemed to have returned to Cambodia. "The voluntariness and extent of these removals may never become known," said the report.

In their new report, *Refuge Denied*, the Lawyers Committee quotes UNBRO reports which state that in the space of two days in January 1987, some 1,683 residents of Site B were moved to Na Trao, 150 miles away. Most of those moved were women who acted as ammunition porters during a period of escalating clashes between the Khmer Rouge and Vietnamese forces.

U.S. Condemnation of the Removals

The US State Department condemned the forced displacements. In a press statement issued on November 14, the Department said:
"We understand that in July and August the Khmer Rouge moved approximately 8,000 people out of Ta Luan Camp in Thailand's Trat Province to an area closer to the Cambodian border called Khao Phlu. Approximately 2,000 Khmer, mostly the aged and infirm, now remain at Ta Luan.

"More recently, we have received reports that similar forced movements of civilians under Khmer Rouge control have occurred in O'Trao and Natrao camps in Surin Province.

17

"We condemn this forced relocation of innocent civilians from the relative safety of UN-assisted camps to more remote areas subject to cross-border shelling and lacking the necessary facilities for the provision of essential services.

"We have urged the Royal Thai government to use its influence to encourage more responsible, humane actions on the part of the Khmer Rouge, and we understand that they have done so."

VIETNAMESE SHELLING

The Khmer Rouge effort to set up new populated areas near or inside the Cambodian border was quashed by Vietnamese and Phnom Penh troops in November 1988 with the heaviest border shelling since 1985. Aid workers in Sok Sann, a KPNLF camp near Ta Luan, said they heard shells falling every three seconds on November 17 and 18 and as often as once a minute for days afterwards. Shelling was more sporadic in the region near O'Trao but also continued for weeks.

"The shelling seems to be coming from anywhere the Khmer Rouge have moved refugees," an aid official with access to the border told Asia Watch in late November 1988.

Asia Watch believes that such long-range shelling, whether by the Vietnamese forces or by the Khmer Rouge itself (see below) is in violation of the laws of war, since there are civilians in the region and those responsible for the shelling cannot distinguish at a distance between military and civilian targets.

Despite the intensity of the shelling, no wounded were evacuated to outside hospitals, and while the Khmer Rouge apparently made use of their own limited medical facilities, they appear to have deliberately denied medical care to some of the injured rather than bring them to the attention of international aid agency staff.

"Everyone wonders why we are not seeing wounded," one official of the International Committee of the Red Cross (ICRC) was quoted as saying. "We assume the wounded are being kept back, that it's an internal decision of the Khmer Rouge."[*]

---

[*]   The New York Times, November 29, 1988.

There is little question that injuries occurred. The KPNLF, which has a military base on a hill about three kilometers from the Khmer Rouge "satellite" camp of V8, reported that both V3 and O'Trao South had been levelled. They reported up to 400 casualties, although that figure could not be confirmed.

Aid officials also discovered through Cambodian sources that the hospital in the closed Khmer Rouge camp 85, a satellite of Site 8 with more than 300 beds, was filled with casualties.* Since they do not have access to the camp, the aid workers could not verify whether all the wounded were from the shelled area around Ta Luan, which is a long way from the closed camp. But refugees who returned to Ta Luan spoke of seeing wounded or dead, including family members. Some said that they had seen Khmer Rouge cadre taking casualties over the border into Cambodia.

One month later, aid workers still did not know the real extent of the damage. "After that kind of sustained, heavy shelling, it would be a miracle if there *weren't* heavy casualties," one Western aid official said in a telephone interview from Aranyaprathet in December, "but without access, we have no way of finding out what really happened."

One result of the pushback by Vietnamese troops was the return of refugees to the evacuated camps. Around the time of the worst shelling in the south, some 3,000 refugees flooded back into Ta Luan. Aid officials said 1,000 or more refugees were also thought to be in the jungles just outside the camp. While UNBRO aid workers passed out blue plastic sheeting for makeshift tents and gave bamboo and thatch to build new houses, Khmer Rouge officials did not ask them to resume food rations. One aid official visiting the camp said that returning refugees looked as though they had been adequately fed, and that the Khmer Rouge seemed to be getting the supplies they needed without UN assistance. Another interviewed by Asia Watch said it was "ominous" that the Khmer Rouge had not requested UN rations for the returnees. "They may not want to go through the

---

*   they do not have access to the camp, the aid workers could not ve

20

hassle of applying if they are only going to keep the refugees here for a short time," he said. In fact, Asia Watch learned in January 1989 that some of those who returned to Ta Luan were forced back toward the border by Khmer Rouge leaders in late December 1988-early January 1989.

HUMAN RIGHTS ABUSES INSIDE
KHMER ROUGE CAMPS

Many of the human rights abuses that characterized the population removals appear to be regular occurrences inside the refugee camps administered by the Khmer Rouge: forced labor, denial of medical care, denial of food as a means of coercion, use of civilians against their will for military purposes, and harsh penalties, including execution, for those who disobey orders.

At a Kampuchea Trust Fund Donor Meeting on June 15, 1988 in Bangkok, the Director of UNBRO, Y.Y. Kim, said, "As regards the camps under [Khmer Rouge] management, we are regularly in receipt of first-hand reports of bizarre violations of human rights from UNBRO staff, ICRC delegates, and voluntary agency personnel."

Summary Executions

There are frequent reports of summary executions and "disappearances" from Khmer Rouge camps, but relatively few are documented.

Two incidents were mentioned by S.A.M.S. Kibria, Special Representative of the Secretary General of the United Nations for Coordination of Kampuchean Humanitarian Assistance Programs, at a September 8, 1988 meeting of aid donors in New York.

He said that reports compiled by ICRC and UNBRO staff cited the summary executions of two men in Site 8 on April 24 and June 25, 1988. Both men had apparently deserted their military units.[*]

The first case involved a man named Moeun Noeun, 30, a Khmer Rouge soldier based at Site 8 South. On April 4 he had come to Site 8 to take part in Khmer New Year celebrations, without the per-

---

[*] The Nation, (Bangkok, Thailand) September 17, 1988.

mission of his camp commander, according to some of the refugees in Site 8. He was said to have stolen weapons from his camp in order to sell them at Site 8 and get money for the New Year. On April 10, one of the commanders from Site 8 South came to summon him home, but Moeun Noeun refused and went into hiding. On April 24, the Khmer Rouge administrators of Site 8 discovered that he was staying at his aunt's house, and at 8:00 that evening, 20-30 armed soldiers surrounded the house. Three soldiers called out to Moeun Noeun to surrender, and when he did not reply, three or four shots were fired into the house. His aunt, her daughter and three children were allowed to leave the house, and four soldiers then entered to arrest Moeun Noeun. They took him outside and immediately executed him. He was shot at point blank range, according to eyewitnesses, once in the bladder, once in the heart and once in the head. Khmer Rouge officials cremated the body early the next morning.

The second case involved a man named Rath who was shot in the back of the head. After rumors of the execution began to circulate in Site 8, aid agency officials together with a Thai army officer began a search for the body. They obtained an exact description of the grave site and on July 8, they discovered the corpse, some one and a half miles south of Site 8.

"These executions have been brought to the attention of the Thai authorities as well as the Khmer Rouge representative, and I hope that firm action would be taken to put an end to such outrageous violations of human rights," Kibria said.

Forced Labor and Portering

Many refugees who have escaped from Khmer Rouge camps tell of being forced to carry arms and ammunition through heavily-mined areas along the border. No distinction is made between military personnel and civilians -- pregnant women and pre-teenage children have been among those forced to act as porters, and refugees say that Khmer Rouge leaders expect all people in their camps to contribute to the war effort with the exception of the very old. Three teenagers living in Ta Luan camp said in January 1989 that they and everyone else in the camp were regarded by camp authorities as part of the military and had to wear the dark green shirts of the Chinese-supplied uniforms of the Khmer Rouge. In some camps, all men and boys are required to wear uniforms.

Insofar as Khmer Rouge leaders have addressed the issue of refugees carrying ammunition into Cambodia, they insist that these people are volunteers. An open letter, allegedly from refugees, was broadcast on Voice of the National Army of Democratic Kampuchea radio on November 29, 1988 saying:

"Some of us have given up spouses and children to serve in the army. Others have volunteered to become porters of provisions and material to the battlefield ... If we, as Cambodians, are not striving for national liberation for ourselves, then who will carry the task for us? ... We shall do it with all our heart and our patriotic sentiments."

In Site 8, Mr. Or Hy, a member of the camp's standing committee, said in November 1988 that refugees spontaneously come to their section leaders and "asked to be allowed to porter."

Of the dozens of refugees who have escaped from Khmer Rouge camps and have since been interviewed by journalists and aid officials, none are known to have said they or anyone else in their camps volunteered for this highly dangerous duty. Aid workers say some refugees still inside the Khmer Rouge camps may indeed have volunteered either because they are Khmer Rouge supporters or because portering allows the opportunity to do black-market trading inside Cambodia when the groups stop at villages. But many of the refugees who have escaped from the Khmer Rouge camps said the opposite. They say they were told their food rations would be cut, or they could be sent to military re-education camps or to jail, if they did not porter -- so they did.

Chan, a 32-year-old man from Battambang province, lost both of his legs while serving as a conscripted Khmer Rouge soldier. He said he was imprisoned by the PRK four years ago for helping the KPNLF. He escaped, planning to join the KPNLF, but encountered the Khmer Rouge on his way to the border.

He said the Khmer Rouge forced him to porter ammunition, but he lost his legs in a land-mine accident when he was cutting down a banana tree. Khmer Rouge soldiers carried him to Borai camp, where he lived in a house with five other amputees. He estimated there to be 400 to 500 amputees in Borai, and said that many lived together in one area.

Chan said he escaped from Borai because he heard that his parents and his brother were in Sok Sann, only a few kilometers away. Chan had not seen his family since the Khmer Rouge took power in 1975 and had given them up for dead. When the Borai camp officials refused to let him move to Sok Sann, Chan said he took two low footstools and, shifting himself from one to the other on the strength of his arms, made his way over hills and through jungle to Sok Sann. "They [the Khmer Rouge camp leaders] saw me leave, but they didn't believe an amputee could run away, so they didn't try to stop me," he said. After two days of travelling, Chan said, he met Thai villagers who told him to wait, that they would go get his brother. His brother came, and took him the final distance to Sok Sann on November 16, 1988.

Som, a 29-year-old woman from Kampong Chenang, said Khmer Rouge soldiers came to her village about a year ago and ordered her to buy rice for them. She said she did so but then was forced to go with the soldiers to the border. She ended up in Kai Che where, she said, she had to porter 10 days at a time, with a three-day break between trips. She said she generally went in a group with 10 other women, most of them between the ages of 24 and 30.

Aing, a 61-year-old man from Kampong Cham, carried the ashes of his son with him from the Khmer Rouge camp of Huay Chan to the Sihanoukist camp of Site 8. He said he left O'Trao because Khmer Rouge leaders there would not let him bury his son, who was killed in battle while serving as a conscripted Khmer Rouge soldier.

Aing left Cambodia with his family in 1983, when the PRK had tried to conscript his son to fight along the border with them. Aing and his family were trying to get to the Site 8, but were intercepted on their way by Khmer Rouge soldiers who took them to Huay Chan. His 22-year-old son was told that if he didn't fight he would be "put in jail with chains on his legs." Aing said he also knew one man whom the Khmer Rouge killed in 1983 because he had refused to fight with the Khmer Rouge and said he supported Sihanouk.

While in Huay Chan, the camp that lost its UNBRO aid in May 1988 after camp leaders refused to allow UNBRO monitoring, Aing said he often did not get enough to eat. He said he went with a group of about 100 other people to steal sweet potatoes and other vegetables from nearby Thai villagers, and that the Thais "got angry" about this. Aing explained that the Khmer Rouge sometimes cut off rice and other food supplies for up to five days at a time, with little explanation. "I could last without rice for two or three days, but then I got hungry, and I had to go out and steal," Aing said.

Describing life in Huay Chan, Aing said all the men wore the green Chinese uniform -- as did all women who portered. The camp had a hospital, but no medicine, he said. Refugees who got sick had to go to the hospital nonetheless or were made to work.

There was one school within the camp, Aing said, aimed at adults. The classes were led by the camp commander, called Pouk, who taught that the Khmer Rouge did not kill any Cambodians while they were in power. Rather, it was the Vietnamese and also Sihanouk and his troops who did the killing. Aing commented that he never saw Sihanouk troops kill anyone in 1975-78, but that he did see Khmer Rouge cadre bludgeon many people to death in Kampong Cham after first making them dig their own graves. He said his own mother died of starvation under the Khmer Rouge and that his aunt and cousin were killed.

Aing's daughter, Sokhorn, was forced to begin portering as soon as she arrived at Huay Chan, at age 15. She said some of her days consisted of nine hours of sharpening *ponji* (pointed sticks designed to impale the enemy).

During five years in the camp, she was forced to make 15 trips through heavily mined mountains carrying the *ponji* -- the last when she was eight months pregnant. She said the trips lasted between a couple of days and a month, and that she usually went with a group of about 30 other women and a guard of armed Khmer Rouge soldiers.

"If I got tired and wanted to stop to rest, I couldn't," she said, recalling how she sometimes staggered under heavy loads of rice, bullets or shells. "The Khmer Rouge told us they would take us to re-education camps and we would be punished."

On almost every trip, Sokhorn said, at least two women were injured by stepping on land mines. She said she also saw five women killed by land mines, and others cut down by Vietnamese and PRK crossfire.

Sokhorn escaped with her husband, her parents, her brother and her eight-month-old daughter to Site 8 in early November 1988.

Another refugee in Site 8, Hin Hon, 25, told a *New York Times* reporter that he was forced to carry Chinese-made ammunition, land mines and mortar shells into Cambodia seven times between March 1987 and October 1988. Hieng Sieng, 41, was conscripted three times for such duty before he managed to escape.*

Sou Chom, 33, was forced to carry B40 rockets into Cambodia. Like many others, he had thought he was joining forces with Sihanouk loyalists when he arrived at a place called Camp 40 controlled by the Khmer Rouge. His two daughters, aged four and seven, died of malaria at the camp for lack of medical attention.**

Cruel and Inhuman Treatment

There appear to be various forms of detention practiced by the Khmer Rouge. Some refugees are sent to re-education camps. Others return from long absences with bruises and wounds that they say are from beatings in "jail."

One of the most vivid accounts of detention comes from a 27-year-old Khmer Krom (an ethnic Khmer from Vietnam) who had served in the South Vietnamese army prior to 1975. About five years ago, Kim fled Vietnam hoping to reach Thailand and from there get to the United States. As he neared the Thai-Cambodian border he was abducted by the Khmer Rouge and forced into service for almost three years. He escaped and reached Site 8 but was captured

---

* The New York Times, November 20, 1988.

** Far Eastern Economic Review, December 1, 1988.

28

by Khmer Rouge soldiers from Site 8 South and detained there for two years.

During his detention, Kim says he was beaten at least eight times with gun butts and wooden sticks. He and seven other prisoners were forced to do heavy labor every day, including digging trenches and carrying mortar shells into Cambodia. He reported that minor offenders were kept chained by one leg to a horizontal bamboo pole. More serious offenders had both legs chained.

Kim Sung escaped from the prison on July 30, 1988. On August 4 he told aid agency officials that he was going to try to return to Site 8 South to rescue other captives there. A week later, he had not returned. Asia Watch does not know what happened to him.

Other people who have escaped from Khmer Rouge prisons have reported that their ankles were shackled together and then chained to other prisoners at night.

In their report *Refuge Denied,* the Lawyers Committee for Human Rights quoted recent escapees as saying that three jails were located outside Site 8, at Pluon Chai, Phnom Dey and Klong Nam Soi, and that few imprisoned there had escaped or returned.[*]

One man told the Lawyers Committee he had been held with nine others in an open area surrounded by land mines. The total number of detainees there was 70, including 10-year-old children. He said beatings were common and some prisoners had died for lack of medical treatment.[**]

In addition to refugees detained for specific offenses, there are thousands in Khmer Rouge camps who are there against their will. Even in Site 8, where conditions are relatively better than in other Khmer Rouge camps, Cambodians have told aid workers that the vast majority of refugees there would prefer to be in a non-Khmer Rouge camp if given the choice. While some of Khmer Rouge camps' populations include those who were loyal to the cadre during their

---

[*]   Refuge Denied, p.75.

[**]   Ibid., p. 70.

rule, or families of such people, many others simply took a road out of Cambodia that led them to a Khmer Rouge-controlled area. In some cases, say refugees who have escaped from northern Khmer Rouge camps to the Site B camp controlled by Sihanouk loyalists, they had been heading for FUNCINPEC camps but were intercepted on their way and taken to a Khmer Rouge camp. FUNCINPEC statistics show that more than 230 refugees have escaped to Site B from Khmer Rouge camps since 1986 -- including 79 in October 1988 alone. KPNLF camp administration of Sok Sann, near the southern Khmer Rouge camps, say they don't have exact statistics but that "many, many" refugees have escaped there from Khmer Rouge camps in the area, especially since the population movement out of Ta Luan.

Restrictions on Basic Freedoms inside the Camps

Khmer Rouge camps have a tight system of social and political control, according to refugees who have escaped from them. Camps are divided into sections, subsections and rows, and refugees are usually confined to their own small areas. Often they do not know the name of the camp they are in or where it is located.

"You can't sneak away, because wherever you'd go outside of your own section, you'd clearly be out of place," one aid worker familiar with Khmer Rouge camps told Asia Watch. "And there are no secrets within each section. Everyone knows everyone, everyone watches everyone. Look around a Khmer Rouge camp, and you'll probably see a lot of people sitting around looking lethargic. It's because they're afraid to do much, because there's so much they could do wrong."

Single men and women are restricted from marrying before a certain age and then only with permission from the camp ad-ministrators. They are told that this is because they are expected to serve the Khmer Rouge cause first before they have families. One refugee who escaped to Sok Sann reported that a neighbor of his in Kai Che, a 22-year-old man named Hoan, was thrown in jail for daring to meet his 21-year-old girlfriend in secret after the Khmer Rouge administration in the camp refused to let them wed. Thai villagers near the jail, on a heavily forested mountain, reported back to Hoan's family in Kai Che that Hoan starved to death in jail.

Listening to any radio broadcasts other than those of the Khmer Rouge is strictly prohibited, say refugees from Site 8, Kai Che, Borai, O'Trao and the now-closed Huay Chan camps.

Refugees are warned not to talk with foreigners and are threatened with punishment if they do. In Site 8, aid sources say, some of the refugees who have disappeared and have not come back are thought to have been singled out for punishment because of their contact with foreign aid workers or journalists.

Refugees at present have no option to transfer out of camps controlled by the Khmer Rouge. Those who have escaped Khmer Rouge control generally have done so during enforced portering inside Cambodia when they have managed to evade their Khmer Rouge guards and find their way back to the Thai border to non-Khmer Rouge camps. The Thai government, for the most part, has maintained a hands-off policy, not questioning what goes on inside Khmer Rouge camps and not allowing refugees who wish to leave to do so.

Exposure to Shelling and Mines

The Khmer Rouge routinely expose civilians to mines and shelling by forcing them to carry materials across the border. But there are also accusations that the Khmer Rouge occasionally have deliberately shelled their own camps and blamed it on the Vietnamese to motivate reluctant refugees to continue to take part in fighting and portering or to punish them for perceived offenses.

In April 1988, for example, a group of Khmer Rouge soldiers entered Site 8 and demanded food from civilians there. The food was late in arriving, and the soldiers in anger fired on Section 13 of the camp. A hand-held rocket launcher was used to fire the shell which left a crater about one meter deep. No one was injured.

A much more serious incident occurred on July 14, 1988 when, without warning, the entire Site 8 population was exposed to shelling. A total of eight shells hit the camp, killing four people and injuring 21. The Khmer Rouge claimed that its troops had attacked a Vietnamese/PRK position on the much-coveted Mountain No.53, about 2.5 miles southeast of Site 8. They said the Vietnamese directly bombed Site 8 in an effort to thwart the attack.

According to several sources, however, the Khmer Rouge authorities in Site 8 felt that the residents there had become unwilling to fight the Vietnamese or carry supplies to the combat zones and wanted to motivate them to fight. They were also thought to be trying to discourage refugees in other Khmer Rouge camps from wanting to live in Site 8, the "showcase" camp, by showing it to be a dangerous and undesirable place.

The kind of shells used appears to support this theory, as 122m shells (which the Khmer Rouge use) rather than 130mm shells (used by the Vietnamese) were found.

The Lawyers Committee report, *Seeking Shelter*, quoted "several well-informed sources" who strongly suspected that these and other incidents of violence were deliberately orchestrated by the Khmer Rouge "to persuade the Thai government that Site 8's population is in danger and therefore should be moved to Phnom Dey or to another location (which presumably would be inaccessible to foreign observers)."*

The report cited three examples. On May 14, 1985, one civilian was killed and several others injured after 30 to 40 Khmer Rouge soldiers ran through the camp, firing guns and rocket-propelled grenades. On October 23, 1985, according to an eye-witness, soldiers ran through the camp shooting, to try and force people to move to Phnom Dey. And on May 29, 1986, a series of shells fell into the middle of Site 8, killing at least 11 refugees and wounding 30 to 50 others, mostly children. According to the report, "The attack occurred on the very day that some civilians living in a military DK [Khmer Rouge] camp were to be transferred to Site 8 -- a move the Khmer Rouge reportedly opposed."**

---

*   Seeking Shelter, p. 75.

**   Seeking Shelter, pp. 75-76.

32

Land mines are a constant hazard along the border, and refugees from Khmer Rouge camps who are forced to porter arms and ammunition into Cambodia are particularly vulnerable.

On September 5, 1988, for example, 150 Cambodian "volunteers" from Site 8 were taken to Phnom Chut by Thai military trucks so that they could take supplies across the border. On September 6, a man in the middle of the group stepped on a mine, incurring grave but non-fatal injuries. A man who had been near him suffered light shrapnel wounds. He was treated at the Site 8 hospital but was afraid to talk openly about the incident. Five days later, another man from Site 8 stepped on a mine and died from loss of blood at a forest southeast of Site 8, according to aid workers.

It is probably not illegal, according to the laws of war, for parties to the conflict to place mines along the border, since the area is considered a military objective by Thai, Cambodian and Vietnamese forces. * But the manner in which the mines are placed may be in violation of the Protocol on Mines which requires that the placement of mines be accurately recorded and that they not be placed so as to "cause incidental loss of civilian life, injury to civilians, damage to civilian objects, or a combination thereof, which would be excessive in relation to the concrete and direct military advantage anticipated."

---

* The use of mines is governed by the Protocol on Prohibitions or Restrictions on the Use of Mines, Booby Traps and Other Devices (Protocol II) annexed to the 1981 UN Convention on Prohibition or Restrictions on the Use of Certain Conventional Weapons Which May be Deemed to be Excessively Injurious and To Have Indiscrimate Effects.

ATTITUDE OF WESTERN AID AGENCIES

Because the Khmer Rouge seem to have a viable alternative means of getting supplies, some Western aid officials have adopted a policy of stepping lightly on such issues as everyday human rights abuses in Khmer Rouge camps. The rationale is that by being allowed to carry out aid programs in Khmer Rouge camps, aid agencies can have some access to refugees, and offer some modicum of protection and outside influence. They say they do not have the necessary leverage to push hard for change in the way refugees are treated; that if they come on too strong the Khmer Rouge will simply bar them from their camps and cut off the refugees' last link with the outside world. By maintaining a presence, international organizations can work to make gradual improvements in the camps, they say.

"If you isolate them and push them back into the jungle, it may make them all the more radical," says one aid official.

Other observers question whether this "one small step at a time" approach has really worked. Although the Khmer Rouge administration has made some concessions, such as allowing a limited number of medical evacuations and negotiating toward an UNBRO-coordinated education program in the camps, such observers say the overall social structure and approach in Khmer Rouge camps has changed very little.

"You won't hear of Khmer Rouge mass murders or even widespread torture like before," said one aid official. "But people disappear during the night ... often with their whole families ... and that's it. You never see them again. Are they killed? Are they just moved to another camp, out of our reach? We don't know. We can't find out."

HUMAN RIGHTS IMPLICATIONS OF THE REMOVALS

Asia Watch believes that the forced population removals and other abuses by the Khmer Rouge are in clear violation of international human rights standards and humanitarian laws on armed conflict.   Common Article 3 of the Geneva Conventions provides,

"In the case of armed conflict not of an international character.... each Party to the conflict shall be bound to apply as a minimum the following provisions:

1) Persons taking no active part in the hostilities, including members of the armed forces who have laid down their arms and those placed *hors de combat* by sickness, wounds, detention, or any other cause, shall in all circumstances be treated humanely, without any adverse distinction founded on race, color, religion or faith, sex, birth or wealth, or any other similar criteria.

To this end, the following acts are and shall remain prohibited at any time and in any place whatsoever with respect to the above-mentioned persons:

a) violence to life and person, in particular murder of all kinds, mutilation, cruel treatment and torture

b) taking of hostages

c) outrages upon personal dignity, in particular, humiliating and degrading treatment

d) the passing of sentences and the carrying out of executions without previous judgment pronounced by a regularly constituted court affording all the judicial guarantees which are recognized as indispensable by civilized people."

The Khmer Rouge practice of forcing teenagers, pregnant women and other civilians against their will to carry supplies into a war zone where they are exposed to mines, shelling and disease violates any concept of "humane treatment" while the summary executions described above are in clear violation of the prohibition against such measures taking place without judicial guarantees.

Denial of Medical Care

The second part of Common Article 3 says, "The wounded and sick shall be collected and cared for."

The denial of medical care to victims of shelling and mines, the prohibition on access by international agencies, the refusal of Khmer Rouge administrators to evacuate refugees in closed camps for medical treatment, and the abandonment of the sick and wounded in the course of the forced population removals of late 1988 are in violation of this provision.

These provisions were designed to ensure that supporters of one side to an armed conflict would be treated humanely by those of the other. But the Khmer Rouge has denied medical care to its own combatants and civilians under its control.

Access to medical treatment appears to be limited to those who have written permission from their section leader. If refugees are considered not to have adequately performed their duties, they may be denied medical care. Even those refugees who are now allowed to be evacuated for medical reasons, including an unprecedented 48 from O'Trao in October 1988, must have this written permission. Frequently such evacuations are too late. On November 9, 1988, a young anemic boy with cerebral malaria came into Ta Luan hospital from one of the outlying Khmer Rouge camps. He died on the spot in his father's arms.

CONCLUSIONS AND RECOMMENDATIONS

As of early February 1989, the Cambodian conflict was rapidly moving toward a new phase, marked by intensive diplomatic activity involving Vietnam and China; Vietnam and Thailand; China and the Soviet Union; and Vietnam, the Cambodian resistance forces, and the ASEAN countries. The focus was on the trade-off between Vietnamese troop withdrawals and a halting of Chinese aid to Khmer Rouge forces, and on the elements of a coalition government. There is a danger that as discussions on the future of Cambodia proceed, the immediate need to safeguard the human rights of Cambodian refugees in Thailand, particularly those in Khmer Rouge-controlled camps, will be overlooked.

Asia Watch believes the following measures are essential to protect those refugees from further abuse:

- *All refugee camps on Thai soil must be made fully accessible to international humanitarian agencies working on the border.*

It is within the power of the Thai government and military to insist on access by these agencies to closed "satellite" camps and to ensure that it takes place. Asia Watch acknowledges that the Thai authorities have begun to take steps in this direction. Those steps must be encouraged. The Khmer Rouge are dependent on Thailand for access to food and arms supplies, and its forces receive logistical support from elements of the Thai military. There is no justification for allowing an estimated 45,000 refugees to remain beyond the reach of any form of international humanitarian assistance.

Access to camps which are now partially or completely closed would ensure that monitoring of population movements can take place, that medical care is provided to those in need, and that allegations of human rights abuses--including torture and summary executions -- can be investigated. The presence of aid workers in these camps might also discourage the practice of forcing refugees to carry arms and ammunition into Cambodia.

International pressure on Thailand to establish and enforce international access to all refugee camps is thus essential.

- *As long as refugee camps in Thailand are administered by different political factions rather than a neutral agency not directly involved in the conflict, refugees must be allowed freedom of choice to transfer from a Khmer Rouge-controlled camp to one controlled by different faction.*

It is clear that many refugees living in Khmer Rouge camps would move elsewhere if they could. In the confusion surrounding the recent attempts by the Khmer Rouge to force thousands of refugees across the border, many refugees took the opportunity to escape. Other refugees have been able to escape by eluding their Khmer Rouge guards while serving as porters of ammunition inside Cambodia and then fleeing back to Thailand to the camps controlled by other factions -- the KPNLF or FUNCINPEC.

If a system allowing freedom of choice is not established soon, there are likely to be further attempts by the Khmer Rouge to move refugees forcibly to areas vacated by the departing Vietnamese troops in order to create "liberated zones" inside Cambodia. Other abuses similar to those documented in this report are also likely to continue as long as refugees can for all practical purposes be held captive by Khmer Rouge camp administrators.

A change in Thai government policy is the first step toward ensuring that refugees do not become in effect captives of a particular political faction. The Thai authorities, in the interests of preserving the Khmer Rouge as a buffer between the Thai military and Vietnamese forces inside Cambodia, have acquiesced in the Khmer Rouge's refusal to let civilians who wish to do so leave camps under its control. *

The continuing Vietnamese troop withdrawals and the progress toward resolving external aspects of the Cambodian conflict have removed this rationale. The international community must now in-

---

* In its January 1989 report on Vietnamese and Cambodian refugees in Thailand, the Lawyers Committee for Human Rights noted that it was told by Western officials in May 1988 that "Thai policy reflected the People's Republic of China's concern that the Khmer Rouge maintain a viable civilian population for political and manpower reasons." See Refuge Denied, p. 78.

40

sist that refugees in Khmer Rouge-controlled camps be allowed to choose whether they wish to remain in those camps or be transferred elsewhere.

- *Planning must start now for the voluntary repatriation of displaced Khmer from Thailand to Cambodia in the context of a settlement. Just as freedom to choose not to live in a camp run by a particular political faction is an essential safeguard for the protection of refugees now, so the freedom to choose to return to Cambodia voluntarily, and not as the captive of a particular faction, is an essential safeguard for the protection of refugees in the future.*

- *The human rights situation in Cambodia and in Cambodian refugee camps in Thailand should be kept under constant review by the United Nations.*

The UN first took up "the situation in Kampuchea" in 1978 when a Special Rapporteur was appointed by the UN Commission on Human Rights to examine extensive allegations of gross violations by the Khmer Rouge after 1975. In 1979 the Special Rapporteur informed the Commission that the Khmer Rouge violations were genocidal in character and the worst to have occurred anywhere in the world since Nazism.

Nonetheless, the Commission declined to take any action, and after 1979, the UN turned its attention to the self-determination questions raised by the Vietnamese intervention. It was not until the 1988 General Assembly that the UN recognized the danger posed by Khmer Rouge participation in a future settlement by calling for a "non-return to the universally-condemned policies and practices of the recent past."

The evidence of continuing abuses by the Khmer Rouge, its military strength, and the recent diplomatic progress toward a settlement justify measures by the UN to monitor human rights practices of all parties to the conflict and ensure that the human rights of all Cambodians will be protected by whatever government eventually emerges in Cambodia.

- *Weapons supply to the Khmer Rouge and the transfer of these weapons across the Thai border into Cambodia should be terminated immediately. It is clear from the forced population move-*

41

ments in late 1988 and from its efforts to stockpile weapons inside Cambodia that the Khmer Rouge is preparing for a protracted war. Continued supply of weapons will only strengthen its ability to do so.

In November 1988, the People's Republic of China, the primary supplier of arms and ammunition to the Khmer Rouge, announced that it would reduce Khmer Rouge supplies as Vietnamese forces withdrew. As movement towards resolution of the conflict continues, there is no rationale for any further supply of arms to the Khmer Rouge.

Just as important as a cessation of arms supply from China, however, is the need to ensure that weapons already in the possession of the Khmer Rouge in Thailand are not allowed to be taken across the border into Cambodia. The Thai military must be urged to cease cooperation with the Khmer Rouge and to prevent the transport of arms and ammunition by forced labor beyond the Thai border.

- *Conditions in Khmer Rouge controlled camps and the forced displacement of refugees in late 1988 underscore the need to prevent those Khmer Rouge leaders most responsible for the Cambodian genocide from playing a further role in Cambodian political life.*

The forced removals took place from camps that were hundreds of kilometers apart, indicating that they were part of a central policy. Such a transfer would not have been attempted without the authorization of leaders like Pol Pot and Ieng Sary who, observers believe, continue to be the primary decision-makers.

Pressure must be exerted by the international community to bring those responsible for crimes against humanity to justice.

- *Each armed party to the Cambodian conflict has been responsible for the placement of land mines which have resulted in incalculable suffering and loss of life. As noted in the beginning of this report, an estimated half million mines are believed to lie around the border. The international community should put pressure on each of these parties to ensure that maps of land mine placement are made available to international humanitarian agencies, and an international effort is mounted to remove these mines and to prohibit any further use of mines along the border.*

Copies of this report are available for $5 from:

Human Rights Watch

36 West 44th Street   1522 K Street, NW
New York, NY 10036   Washington, DC 20005
(212)   840-9460   (202)   371-6592